Barnes & Noble® Reader's

The Art of War

BARNES & NOBLE® READER'S COMPANION™
Today's take on tomorrow's classics.

FICTION
THE CORRECTIONS by Jonathan Franzen
I KNOW WHY THE CAGED BIRD SINGS by Maya Angelou
THE JOY LUCK CLUB by Amy Tan
THE LOVELY BONES by Alice Sebold
THE POISONWOOD BIBLE by Barbara Kingsolver
THE RED TENT by Anita Diamant
WE WERE THE MULVANEYS by Joyce Carol Oates
WHITE TEETH by Zadie Smith

NONFICTION
THE ART OF WAR by Sun Tzu
A BRIEF HISTORY OF TIME by Stephen Hawking
GUNS, GERMS, AND STEEL by Jared Diamond
JOHN ADAMS by David McCullough

BARNES & NOBLE® READER'S COMPANION™

SUN-TZU'S
The Art of War

BARNES
& NOBLE
BOOKS

EDITORIAL DIRECTOR John Kestler
EXECUTIVE EDITOR Ben Florman
DIRECTOR OF TECHNOLOGY Tammy Hepps

SERIES EDITOR John Crowther
MANAGING EDITOR Vincent Janoski

WRITER John Henriksen
EDITOR Matt Blanchard
DESIGN Dan O. Williams, Matt Daniels

Copyright © 2003 by SparkNotes LLC

Cover photograph *Untitled* by Alberto Burri, copyright © Burstein Collection/Corbis

All rights reserved. No part of this book may be used or reproduced in any manner whatsoever without the written permission of the Publisher.

This edition published by Spark Publishing

Spark Publishing
A Division of SparkNotes LLC
120 Fifth Avenue, 8th Floor
New York, NY 10011

Any book purchased without a cover is stolen property, reported as "unsold and destroyed" to the Publisher, who receives no payment for such "stripped books."

ISBN 1-58663-855-6

Library of Congress Cataloging-in-Publication Data available upon request

Printed and bound in the United States

Contents

A TOUR OF THE BOOK an overview of the book 1
Beyond the Battlefield Though its lessons are framed in ancient military terms, *The Art of War* is a priceless guide to the daily decisions of modern life.

POINTS OF VIEW a conversation about *The Art of War* 11
Making the Connections Having read Sun Tzu's words, how can we go about applying them to the questions and conflicts we face today?

A WRITER'S LIFE Sun Tzu's story 39
The Man Behind the Myth Sun Tzu himself remains shrouded in mystery, with some historians going so far as to question whether he existed at all.

THE WORLD OUTSIDE China in the sixth century B.C. 45
Dawning of a New Age China in Sun Tzu's time was in the midst of sweeping change, as ancient traditions fell victim to a new push toward practicality.

A BRIEF HISTORY how readers have used *The Art of War* 51
The 2000-Year Bestseller Originally a secret publication for an emperor's eyes alone, *The Art of War* has become popular reading for millions.

EXPLORE books to consider reading next 55
Other Books of Interest Interested in learning more about Sun Tzu? There's plenty to read, ranging from the academic to the thoroughly practical.

Barnes & Noble® Reader's Companion™

WITH INTELLIGENT CONVERSATION AND ENGAGING commentary from a variety of perspectives, Barnes & Noble Reader's Companions are the perfect complement to today's most widely read and discussed books.

○ ○ ○

Whether you're reading on your own or as part of a book club, Barnes & Noble Reader's Companions provide insights and perspectives on today's most interesting reads: What are other people saying about this book? What's the author trying to tell me?

○ ○ ○

Pick up the Barnes & Noble Reader's Companion to learn more about what you're reading. From the big picture down to the details, you'll get today's take on tomorrow's classics.

BARNES & NOBLE® READER'S COMPANION™

The Art of War

A TOUR OF THE BOOK

Beyond the Battlefield

Though its lessons are framed in ancient military terms, *The Art of War* is a priceless guide to the daily decisions of modern life.

○ ○ ○

TRY MAKING THIS CLAIM to a friend or coworker: a Chinese military manual written more than 2,000 years ago is a hot seller today. When they call you crazy, tell them that the work is *The Art of War* by the obscure genius Sun Tzu. The book isn't an oddity of interest solely to scholars of ancient history—in fact, it's currently marketed to the general public across the globe in countless editions and translations. It reportedly has influenced people as diverse as Japanese industrialists, American MBA students, Napoleon, and certain members of the Nazi high command.

The Art of War is perhaps the greatest perennial bestseller in history, and its reputation is still growing as it enters its third millennium. Businesspeople are drawn to its readability, its ability to distill knowledge about large-scale leadership maneuvers—whether of market forces or military ones—into a few pithy, practical statements.

But the appeal of *The Art of War* extends to others as well. It's so lofty in spirit, so illuminated by a gentle and radiant wisdom, that many readers who have nothing to do with either warfare or business find it simply a useful guide to life. It has a lot to say about the importance of self-knowledge, of being cool-headed in moments of crisis, of understanding one's competitors or opponents, and of valuing spiritual victories more than physical ones.

STRUCTURE AND GENRE OF THE WORK

As rewarding as *The Art of War* is in the long run, it's not an easy work to process quickly. Scattered in its insights, it presents us with a dazzling kaleidoscope of ideas rather than a careful argument that moves logically from one point to another. Many believe the best way to absorb Sun Tzu's ideas is to read a little bit every day, instead of all at once.

The Art of War is divided into thirteen sections with clear titles like "Planning Offensives" and "Employing Spies"—but the content rarely conforms in any strict sense to those titles (which were added by later commentators). Often, a section refers to its title topic once or twice and then flows on to other matters. While many generations of Chinese traditionalists have tried to prove that there's a subtle logic and coherence beneath the apparent looseness, *The Art of War* is bound to frustrate anyone seeking concrete or well-reasoned arguments.

In fact, it may be a misnomer to call *The Art of War* a military manual or treatise on warfare in the first place. Instead, it might make more sense to read it as a philosophical-religious poem about the Tao—the Way—that underlies Chinese Taoism. In this light, Sun Tzu's military subject matter is just one of the forms through which the Tao happens to express itself. The effect is distinctly spiritual, and many readers come away from the work with a strange impression of having received guidance for the soul.

Sun Tzu's career is wrapped up in his writing, and we should always keep in mind the man behind the work. Newer translations of *The Art of War*, such as Ralph D. Sawyer's, stress the author's personality by prefacing each section with the phrase "Sun Tzu said . . .". This lead-in reminds us that *The Art of War* isn't an objective set of scientific statements like the laws of gravity, but the verbal product of human vision and human wisdom. It's as individual—and universal—as the messages of other sages and prophets throughout history. It's less a textbook than a sermon on the mount. Indeed, *The Art of War* even has the look of a religious text: its brief statements are set apart from each other, resembling the often scattershot and unconnected sayings of Jesus. Like New Testament parables, *The Art of War* expects us to use our intuition and life's wisdom to grasp its meaning. Its teaching isn't for the rational mind alone but for the heart and soul as well.

A Tour of the Book

SPIRITUALITY AND THE ART OF LEADERSHIP

Virtually anyone today can benefit from Sun Tzu's practical spirituality. His attention to the spirit is realistic and strategic, not otherworldly and religious. In this day and age, many of us regard spirituality as incompatible with real-world efficiency and productivity—but for Sun Tzu the two go hand in hand. Like Socrates' famous epigram "know thyself," *The Art of War* emphasizes the inner sources of wisdom: you have to get a handle on yourself before you can hope to fulfill your ambitions. Self-knowledge is one of the key elements of successful leadership.

But while many of the Greek philosophers disdained worldly things in their search for a higher vision, Sun Tzu connects his higher vision directly to power and effectiveness in the world of men, governments, and armies. A close relation exists between the soul and the social arena, so a solid self-understanding makes you a force to be reckoned with. It will make you stronger not just in your personal life, but can also be the difference between success and disaster for entire groups and populations.

In a military example, Sun Tzu points out that a temper fit in a general on the battlefield, unlike a spat between lovers, can produce irreversibly bad consequences: "The ruler cannot mobilize the army out of personal anger. . . . Anger can revert to happiness, annoyance can revert to joy, but a vanquished state cannot be revived, the dead cannot be brought back to life." An insight into why you get angry—and act out of irrational anger—could mean the difference between success and failure. In short, your spiritual and psychological side isn't just a private matter for personal reflection or diary writing. It's crucial in a social sense, and if you're an important public figure, it might even prompt the rise or fall of nations.

But self-knowledge encompasses far more than just the personality of the leader—it includes all the forces and resources he commands, be they soldiers fighting for him or a team of sales reps selling his product out in the field. A leader should view the forces he commands as if they were a part of him.

Indeed, Sun Tzu often treats the powers of the leader and the powers of his troops as indistinguishable. The line between psychological strength and military strength becomes blurred. This idea supports Sun

3

The Art of War

Tzu's overall point that spiritual well being in the leader is key to the success of his large-scale endeavors. In the Chinese culture of Sun Tzu's time, this association of an entire army with its leader was somewhat commonplace. It was linked to a "paternalist" idea of rule in which a ruler was to his country as a father is to his children. A ruler had full authority over his subjects and a symbolic identification with them. Sun Tzu states this outright, saying that when the general "regards the troops as his beloved children, they will be willing to die with him."

In short, Sun Tzu teaches us that a sense of familial bonds ensures commitment. It identifies the leader with those he's leading, in both name and spirit. In Sun Tzu's time, the military manpower of a ruler, from his slaves to his family members, was considered part of his property. This manpower was virtually an extension of the ruler and a reflection of his glory. State and army were united with the radiant figure of the ruler himself. The general and his troops were similarly indistinguishable. Sun Tzu often makes this point explicitly: "The general is the supporting pillar of his state. . . . If the supporting pillar is marked by fissures, the state will invariably grow weak."

> A sense of **familial bonds** ensures **commitment.** It **identifies the leader** with those he's leading, in both **name** and **spirit.**

As goes the man, so goes his nation. Because the ruler is an image of his state, his self-understanding must be bound up with an understanding of the people he rules. In this day and age, we might consider self-knowledge as a detailed understanding of the people who work with us or for us in the office. Answering the question "How am I doing?" in the workplace would thus require knowledge of how *they* are doing as well.

Sun Tzu views this psychological connection between general and army—or between any individual and any group—as a spiritual phenomenon. He urges us to associate ourselves deeply with the larger group we're part of, whether in the military, in the business world, or in everyday life.

One of the quirks Sun Tzu uses to blur the line between the individual and the group is that he purposely fails to specify whether he is talking personally or militarily, individually, or collectively. When Sun Tzu writes, "One who knows when he can fight, and when he cannot fight, will be victorious," he uses the word "he" to refer to more than a private, personal readiness on the part of the leader. Here, as throughout *The Art of War*, "he" means "he and his troops" or "he and those he leads." Knowing when the leader is ready to fight is more or less the same as knowing when his men are ready to fight. The leader is a pivotal figure, but his importance as an individual is less than that of the entire system he is a part of.

At the climactic end of the third section of *The Art of War*, Sun Tzu sums up his ideas on offensive strategies with a private, introspective statement that could have come from the mouth of the philosopher Socrates. Sun Tzu writes, "Thus it is said that one who knows the enemy and knows himself will not be endangered in a hundred engagements." Here again, we're not sure whether "himself" means the leader's own personal position or that of the men under his command. Sun Tzu wants us to see these two aspects as so deeply connected that it becomes useless to try to separate them.

In the spiritual synergy of teamwork, there's little difference between understanding your position and understanding the workings of the rest of your organization. In a modern context, we're reminded of the view of Japanese business culture that a business leader or CEO is personally responsible to all of his employees. Sun Tzu's insights are refreshing in these times of growing frustration in American business, when a number of notable CEOs have walked away from corrupt and failing corporations with huge severance packages without any seeming commitment to the employees and shareholders they once led. In this business climate, Sun Tzu's emphasis on fully belonging to your people is good to keep in mind.

THE GENTLE WARRIOR

One of the most surprising aspects of *The Art of War* is its overriding sense of restraint and minimalism—another spiritual touch that has important implications in our world today. Though it may seem paradoxical in a military manual, Sun Tzu's disdain for wanton and bloodthirsty aggression is a major part of his philosophy of war. To sum it up in the author's own words, "subjugating the enemy without fighting is the true pinnacle of excellence."

Western military manuals often take it for granted that warfare is about attack, offering the best ways to plan and execute offensives. But Sun Tzu conceives of fighting as a purer and higher activity. Many martial arts disciplines teach the student how to get the greatest physical effect from the smallest physical exertion. In the same way, Sun Tzu presents the ideal war as a triumph without actually fighting battles at all. Skirmishes, ambushes, and espionage are all preferable to massive confrontation. As Sun Tzu says, "[O]ne who excels at employing the military subjugates other people's armies without engaging in battle, cap-

> *"The ruler cannot mobilize the army out of personal anger. The general cannot engage in battle because of personal frustration."*

tures other people's fortified cities without attacking them, and destroys other people's states without prolonged fighting."

Sun Tzu's basic point is that the best way to conquer is not to destroy the enemy, but—as contradictory as it might seem—to preserve him. He writes, "Preserving [the opponent's] army is best, destroying their army second-best. Preserving their battalions is best, destroying their battalions second-best." The seek-and-destroy strategy key to many Western military strategies is, for Sun Tzu, merely a second-best option. In purely military terms, it's better to see enemies alive and intact in their still-thriving capital than to see them annihilated. The excellent leader "must fight under Heaven with the paramount aim of 'preservation'." Sun Tzu's addition of the phrase "under Heaven" reminds us of his belief that spirituality and hard-nosed leadership skills go hand in hand. There's nothing passive or resigned about Sun Tzu's religious mindset: Heaven wants us to win.

All this emphasis on preserving the enemy causes us to redefine our very notion of what a victory is. With the simplicity of genius, Sun Tzu openly challenges the idea that a great general will attain great triumphs.

If a grandiose victory depletes the state coffers and exhausts the workforce, then such a victory looks like a defeat. A costly victory should be avoided in favor of a live-and-let-live policy.

Sun Tzu takes care to point out the hidden costs of prolonged campaigns. He scorns tactics and maneuvers that require huge investments of time and resources. Careless or misguided planning can lead to significant wastes of time and energy. With his typical scorn for the fiery and unreflective leader, Sun Tzu mocks the commander who "cannot overcome his impatience but instead launches an assault wherein his men swarm over the walls like ants," thus killing a third of his men and failing to take the city. In general, aggressive assaults spell trouble for Sun Tzu. They entail wastes of manpower, time, and resources that make a final "victory" worthless.

Sun Tzu's preference for conceptual triumphs over aggressive ones has a clear relevance to the business world. One company carrying out a hostile takeover of another will find no victory in destroying what it aims to conquer. A healthy and profitable acquisition is worth much more than a ruined one: "The army values being victorious; it does not value prolonged warfare." A real victory will preserve the enemy and spare the costs of battle in the bargain.

A PRACTICAL VISION OF LEADERSHIP

Sun Tzu is a steadfast pragmatist. He has little interest in patriotism or emotionalism—so little, in fact, that flag-wavers may balk at the lack of "higher motivations" in *The Art of War*. Although Sun Tzu writes at length about the psychological states of soldiers and commanders, he never focuses on love of one's nation as a motivation for military valor. He throws in tidbits about how a general who loves his men as his children will inspire them to fight to the death, but the dynamic is one of parent-worshipping more so than pure patriotism or clan loyalty.

Sun Tzu sees the flashy trappings of an army—drums and flags and so on—with a practical eye. Modern Western military thinking often views these articles as tools to whip up the patriotic consciousness of the soldiers. Sun Tzu explains that flags were originally created not for emotional reasons but for logistical ones. For Sun Tzu, flags and pennants are simply devices to ensure that the soldiers will remain aware of each other's presence—a completely mechanical purpose. There's no mention of inspiring a fighting spirit or stirring up patriotic fervor with a good drumbeat and some colorful flags. Radically unsentimental, Sun Tzu always attends to the harder facts.

> Sun Tzu means *The Art of War* to be a **handbook**, a practical manual for strategy and leadership, not a **moral** treatise.

We might be surprised to notice that Sun Tzu is also unconcerned with ethics. We shouldn't misinterpret Sun Tzu's close link to Chinese spirituality as a sign that he's interested in the moral dos and don'ts of war. He never once raises the questions of whether a given war is justified or not, whether the people suffer unfairly when a ruler pursues a military aim, or whether the killing of enemy soldiers is morally defensible. His spirituality focuses on the balanced vision and self-control of the commander—not on whether he is a villain. It's easy to miss the omission of moral questions in *The Art of War*. Sun Tzu's coverage of the ins and outs of war and leadership is so full and rich in other ways that we hardly notice that ethical remarks are missing.

How are we supposed to interpret this complete lack of ethical concern? We might see it as the product of a thoroughly amoral thinker who cares nothing for the ethical consequences of a commander's actions. But the refusal to discuss right and wrong in *The Art of War* doesn't necessarily suggest that Sun Tzu is a monster who advocates success at any cost. Instead, it might mean that Sun Tzu simply doesn't believe that ethical questions are within his realm—he means *The Art of War* to be a handbook, a practical manual for strategy and leadership, not a moral treatise. We shouldn't expect *The Art of War* to offer moral commentary any more than we should expect a textbook on airplane mechanics to tell us when airplanes should and shouldn't be used to drop bombs in wartime. Sun Tzu is interested in explaining *how* certain results are achieved—not *whether or not* they should be achieved.

A Tour of the Book

We can best understand Sun Tzu's spirituality as a higher, transcendent form of practicality. In Western thought, practicality and spirituality are often imagined to be opposites. But in Chinese thought they are intertwined: a true mastery of the soul is said to bring about a heightened effectiveness in everyday life. Thus, in *The Art of War*, the lofty dreamer who speaks of Heaven and self-knowledge doesn't contradict the shrewd pragmatist who knows how long it takes to build defense structures—they're two sides of the same man.

Sun Tzu's concern for practical details sometimes tiptoes into the realm of minutia. He tells us that if we see dust rising up in a sharply defined column, we know that chariots are coming. But if the cloud is low and broad, it's infantry approaching. If birds suddenly take flight, an ambush is in the works. Psychological cues are just as important. Hanging cooking utensils suggest that the enemy army is too tired to carry out daily functions like meal preparation. If enemy troops congregate in scattered groups, then the solidarity of the masses has been lost. A commander who frequently imposes punishments is probably having great difficulty, as is one who grants noticeably frequent rewards. If officers are angry, they're exhausted.

Reading this endless laundry list of practical tips from the vantage point of the twenty-first century, we might wonder what lessons we could possibly take from tales of dust clouds and enemy dishware. But although the details of an ancient Chinese military campaign are a far cry from the details of modern-day political campaigns or hostile takeovers, *attention* to these tiny details is important in any arena. In the end, Sun Tzu leaves us with the lesson that even the greatest spiritual master on the battlefield never loses his concern for the little facts, the tiny details. The true spiritual master doesn't deny practical matters—he lifts them to a higher understanding of reality.

This last point is important in interpreting Sun Tzu's work. Sun Tzu doesn't speculate about the big questions of existence in the way that Jesus, Buddha, Plato, and others did. Those readers who approach *The Art of War*

Paths to enlightenment
During the time Sun Tzu was writing *The Art of War,* the Hebrew Torah was being composed, Socrates was teaching in Athens, and the Buddha was showing the path to transcendence in India.

The Art of War

as if they're climbing a mountain to hear a grand old Chinese sage dispensing precious words on the meaning of life will probably be disappointed. Sun Tzu skips over questions about higher meaning almost entirely. But for those who answer their meaning-of-life questions in other ways, who come to Sun Tzu looking for spiritually sophisticated practical guidance on achieving goals in both war and life, *The Art of War* will prove a rewarding experience.

POINTS OF VIEW

Making the Connections

Having read Sun Tzu's words, how can we go about applying them to the questions and conflicts we face today?

○ ○ ○

How can we profit from reading *The Art of War* without being a military or business leader? Can everyday people find something of value in the work too?

FORGET THE SWORDS AND CHARIOTS

The beauty of *The Art of War* is that, while it's disguised as a military strategy manual, its precepts are so abstract that we can use them in the strategy of everyday life as well. The Taoism that underlies leadership maneuvers in *The Art of War* is the same Taoism that millions of ordinary people have relied on through the centuries to live their lives and confront ordinary challenges. War is only one field to which Sun Tzu applies his Taoism. Battle is his extended *example* of the doctrine—not the doctrine itself, which relates to all of existence. We could almost call his work *The Art of Living* and do no injustice to its basic message or purpose.

Even the most ardent pacifist can benefit from seeing warfare as a metaphor for our lives in one way or another. Like any military commander, we are involved in dynamic situations, not static ones. Our lives aren't stationary, but in ceaseless movement. Our lives are not where we're standing now, but the path—the Tao, in Sun Tzu's terms—that is leading us somewhere. If we can grasp the path clearly, we can live more effectively. The terrain of our lives is constantly changing as we move through it.

The military metaphor also reminds us that the movement of life is conflict-ridden. Like a military commander, we always face new obstacles. In many of our lives, conflict (in whatever form) is the norm rather than the exception. Passivity is not an option. Confrontation is unavoidable. We can't curl up and hope for the best any more than a general can retreat to his tent at the peak of battle.

> **The Tao can refer to the way we do things as much as it can refer to the direction in which we go.**

Sun Tzu's military framework urges us to think about our successes and failures actively, in terms of circumstances that to a large extent we can control. Although a good general realizes that there are factors on the battlefield he can't dictate, he also knows that there are many he *can* control. Similarly, we are well advised to remember that we aren't merely the playthings of fate, our success dependent on the whims of random fortune. Rather, our success is up to us and to our abilities to think fast and plan strategically.

Of course, we don't need to go overboard in applying Sun Tzu's military thinking to our everyday lives. We won't gain much from imagining our less-than-favorite coworkers as actual enemies to be defeated. Instead, the military framework of *The Art of War* can encourage us to think more proactively about our goals, our obstacles, and how to surmount those obstacles and attain our goals.

Rather than sit back and wait for a promotion at work, we can view that promotion as the "enemy territory" to be won. We should ask ourselves what's standing in the way of our getting it. Maybe a supervisor or manager isn't convinced that we can handle more responsibility. In that case, the "enemy" is the supervisor's mistaken impression—not the supervisor as a person. The "battle" is correcting our supervisor's view of us by proving ourselves, and we must summon to that battle all the resources at our command. As Sun Tzu emphasizes again and again, knowledge is

Points of View

key: we have to gather all available information about the position we aim for, who held it in the past, and who holds it now. We must judge the "terrain" as a factor in our calculations. Is the general environment at the office a difficult one in which to wage a battle of this sort? Is it appropriate for direct struggle, or does it contain hiding places from which ambushes are possible? Finally, we must maintain a cool and impersonal attitude toward our ambitions. It might be easy to get emotionally invested in the idea of a promotion, but Sun Tzu advises that passion has no place in formulating an effective strategy. We must keep cool, stay rational, and analyze our aims, our obstacles, and the Tao that can help us get what we want.

○ ○ ○

Sun Tzu refers often to "the Tao." What is this exactly, and what does it have to do with strategy?

A TOUGH NUT TO CRACK

Although the word "Tao" gets tossed around pretty liberally in our culture, few of us probably have a firm grip on what exactly the word means. Debates rage among scholars of Chinese culture about how to translate the word "Tao" into English. In the context of *The Art of War*, scholars disagree about how to relate Taoism to Sun Tzu's work.

We know at least that Sun Tzu's frequent references to the Tao point to his considerable debt to the Chinese philosopher Lao-tzu. "Master Lao" (Sun Tzu is "Master Sun") lived a century or so before Sun Tzu. Lao-tzu's ideas are recorded in his influential work of spiritual thought, the *Tao Te Ching*. This work has had an enormous impact on Chinese culture for the past 2,500 years, and has made the term "Tao" familiar to Western laypeople today. But while many have heard the term in common usage, whether they could define it clearly or accurately is a different story.

Most scholars prefer to leave the word in the original Chinese—which hardly helps clarify matters, though the Chinese word does radiate an exotic appeal. Those who do attempt to translate Tao into English often opt for "the Way." This word choice emphasizes the progressive nature of Tao and its extension over time, just as a road or path extends over space. The Tao isn't a static state, but something that *takes* us to new places.

Sun Tzu's first reference to the Tao is virtually synonymous with a "path" that leads either to well-being or to ruination: "Warfare is . . . the Way (Tao) to survival or extinction." The idea of the path emphasizes our free choice in deciding whether or not to follow it. This Taoist spin on battle focuses the enormous honor and burden of free will on the leader, who has the power to shape the fate of both his organization and himself. Moreover, the idea of a freely chosen path implies freely chosen techniques and tricks we use to advance on it. We exercise our free will in following certain strategies that take us where we aim to go. Thus Sun Tzu's use of "Tao" sometimes makes the word sound as if it means "technique" or "application"—as in his famous pronouncement, "Warfare is the Way (Tao) of deception." After all, deception isn't so much a path to follow as a strategy to be applied in advancing on our path. In this light, we see that the Tao can refer to the *way* we do things as much as it can refer to the direction in which we go.

But the Tao is more than a name for the life paths we choose to follow. It has cosmic and moral dimensions as well. It carries a sense of "harmony" or "naturalness," a reference the way things are supposed to be, both universally and socially. Thus Sun Tzu describes the Tao in the third paragraph of *The Art of War* as a kind of harmonious interaction between the ruler and the people he governs: "The Tao causes the people to be fully in accord with the ruler. [Thus] they will die with him; they will live with him and not fear danger." This definition of the Tao is more political than the first one because it embraces more than the survival or extinction of one individual. The entire state is at stake, and the path the leader follows is also the path of the population he drags along behind him. Ralph D. Sawyer emphasizes this political dimension of the Tao—downplaying its spiritual importance—by claiming that the term is basically a shorthand reference to all administrative and juridical procedures canonized by Chinese tradition. This idea of Tao is secular and down-to-earth. It connotes all the political and social consequences of a philosophy of warfare, however spiritual it may be.

Points of View

The Tao can also refer to the inner logic of things, or the analyzable deep reality of a situation. In the eleventh section of *The Art of War*, Sun Tzu says that the "Tao of the invader" is the idea that when you advance deeply into enemy territory, your troops will automatically "cling together." Sun Tzu means that this is simply the way it is—it's logical that a successful invasion is unifying. Thus the Tao here is another name for the natural order of things. In other places, Sun Tzu emphasizes the natural order as it is uncovered by careful intellectual activity. In section ten of *The Art of War*, the "Tao of terrain" represents the way that a general must select and then exploit the "configuration" of the terrain in order to create the battle that's best for him. In this case, the Tao is the set of questions we must run through in making our assessment of the lay of the land. Unlike the spiritual and political definitions of Tao, this sense of it emphasizes rational analysis and careful intellectual work.

We should consider all these different interpretations of the Tao to be interrelated aspects of one idea, like facets of a diamond, rather than a hodgepodge of conflicting definitions. They're more harmonious than they appear at first, since the common denominator in all of them is "procedure." There's a proper way to do things, and consequently a proper way to engage in warfare. It leads to success for both the individual leader and the masses he commands and governs. The wise person freely chooses this procedure, though it's larger than any individual because it is a kind of cosmic force of rightness. It embraces several techniques, including a rational analysis of the situation at hand. It carries with it the understanding that beneath the flurry on the battlefield there's a truth to be grasped, and that this truth can be used to determine effective action.

There are still conflicting views among scholars as to whether or not *The Art of War* is really a Taoist philosophical work. One recent translator of Sun Tzu, Thomas Cleary, argues that *The Art of War* is a full-fledged application of Taoist spiritual principles to the practice of warfare. But others, like Ralph D. Sawyer, stress the hard-nosed, practical side of Sun Tzu and downplay his flirtation with abstract spiritual themes. But it may be that both scholarly opinions are right, that Sun Tzu's Taoism doesn't prevent him from being a pragmatist in everyday matters.

The Art of War

Isn't charisma a valuable characteristic in a leader? Why does Sun Tzu have so little to say about it?

CHARM ISN'T EVERYTHING

Sun Tzu's thoughts on a leader's personality are among the most innovative insights in *The Art of War*. Military theorists in the Western world—and many of us generally—tend to associate a strong personality with good leadership. When we think of great military commanders, we think of men with strong force of character, like Alexander the Great or Napoleon, who made themselves into myths and enticed whole generations of schoolboys to imitate them.

But this thought is misleading. Even Western history is full of successful generals with nondescript personalities and no great charisma to speak of. We don't hear about them as often, because it's harder to make stirring biographies and films about them. But they were just as successful relative to world history as the flashier leaders—and in some cases more so.

In short, there's no irrefutable evidence that good leadership requires overflowing personal charisma. Indeed, corporate culture in these first years of the twenty-first century has already offered some notorious examples of charismatic CEOs who have led their companies to ruin. Beyond corporate life, Sun Tzu's advice on being an effective leader is useful to ordinary folks as well—to all of us trying to marshal our resources and achieve our goals on the battlefield of life. As part of this effort, we have to rethink what a good leader is.

One of Sun Tzu's great achievements in *The Art of War* is to offer an alternative vision of leadership—as something that's individual and creative but not based on character, personal charm, or an ability to seduce the masses into hero worship. Instead, Sun Tzu values a more withdrawn and mysterious personality, preferring the leader who lingers backstage to the leader who hogs the limelight and soaks up the applause of his troops. A good commander's presence should be felt everywhere—but through his vital force and wise decisions rather than through press conferences and star turns.

Points of View

In fact, Sun Tzu has nothing to say about how a leader should present himself to his subordinates. He writes as if the matter were irrelevant to him. He recommends that the leader keep his plans a secret even from his own men, avoiding "town hall" informational meetings entirely. Transparency and open lines of communication have no place in *The Art of War*. Interestingly, Sun Tzu draws most of his metaphors for effective armies from forces that don't have any leaders at all—the forces of nature. When he compares a strong army to a forest and a river, we realize that his idea of leadership is so subtle and organic as to force us to reassess what we mean by the term "leader."

For Sun Tzu, a forceful personality is a dangerously unreliable thing. Personal charisma often comes hand in hand with emotion and passion, which makes it susceptible to corruption and irrationality. Fame, for instance, is dangerous. Whereas other theorists of war value hunger for fame as an incentive for valor, Sun Tzu believes it interferes with the rational analysis of the situation. It focuses the commander's attention on his own self-image rather than on strategies for success: "[A general] who does not advance to seek fame . . . but seeks only to preserve the people and gain advantage for the ruler is the state's treasure." Any decision based on concern for the leader rather than concern for the effective actions of the troops is risky and should be avoided. Whenever Sun Tzu mentions ambition or anger in a general, he does so negatively, as a warning or a prohibition: "The ruler cannot mobilize the army out of personal anger. The general cannot engage in battle because of personal frustration. . . . Anger can revert to happiness, annoyance can revert to joy, but a vanquished state cannot be revived, the dead cannot be brought back to life." Sun Tzu's negative perspective on the "personal" here is clear.

We shouldn't take the fact that Sun Tzu downplays personal charisma in leadership to mean that he imagines effective leaders to be robot-like figures in penthouse offices, distant from the hearts of those they lead. On the contrary, Sun Tzu hints that leaders should elicit warm feelings from their subjects. Though he never dwells on this idea, he does make an offhand comment that implies that the ideal relations between the people and their leader can be as intimate as family bonds: "When the general regards his troops as young children, they will advance into the deepest valleys with him. When he regards the troops as his beloved children, they will be willing to die with him." It seems an odd idea from our perspective, for most modern-day leaders would probably consider such a view condescending and obnoxious.

But Sun Tzu's point sheds light on his idea of leadership. A leader who is a father figure is very different from a center-stage superstar leader. A successful father figure inspires deep trust, devotion, and commitment, while a superstar inspires hero worship. The father figure doesn't have to worry about his image as the charismatic hero does, because he knows that his inferiors' faith in him goes far deeper than simple adoration. Perhaps most important, the father figure genuinely *cares* about his children, just as a proper general or business leader should care about his underlings—not just feign concern for them, but really take a committed interest in advancing their well-being. And, like any good father, he doesn't do so for the sake of the fame he will receive for it.

Sun Tzu's image of the leader is thus not that of a depersonalized, machine-like administrator. It's warm and deeply human. But leadership isn't a cult of personality and shouldn't be based on the commander's charms or the troops' worship of a larger-than-life superhero. Sun Tzu prefers a quieter, more hidden, but still active and watchful form of leadership. The commander acts behind the scenes, "unfathomable," just as a father provides for his children by working at a job that his small children probably don't understand—and don't have to understand. Sun Tzu's ideal leader is a strict, wise, and guiding presence who doesn't have to present a flashy façade in order to gain respect and obedience. Rather, he lets his proper actions earn the loving trust of his inferiors.

Points of View

Wise leadership is key, but a leader is only as effective as those under his command. What does Sun Tzu say about keeping the troops motivated and in good fighting spirit?

THREE WORDS: SHARE THE WEALTH

Sun Tzu knows how important it is to keep up your staff's morale and their readiness to fight valiantly, but he differs from others in his opinions on what accomplishes that goal. He glosses over the motivators that other military theorists of past and present have championed—slogans, flags, songs, logos, and the like. Sun Tzu never criticizes these inspirational paraphernalia directly, but his silence on the subject stands out. He has nothing to say about firing up the soldiers with sentimental ideas about their homeland. He doesn't instruct us to make the soldiers wage bold war in the name of the king or the royal family. Sun Tzu does mention flags and pennants at one point, but he regards them only in the most practical sense, as a way to keep all the soldiers in pace with one another: "Gongs, drums, pennants, and flags are the means to unify the men's ears and eyes." It's a far cry from the flag-waving troop-rallying we're used to seeing in popular culture. In contrast, Sun Tzu's lack of sentimentality is refreshingly realistic.

But Sun Tzu is quick to point out that cash succeeds where patriotism fails. Songs and slogans might not stir up the troops effectively, but wealth does. Sun Tzu is explicit and direct about the value of profit sharing as a way to get people fighting: "When you plunder a district, divide the wealth among your troops. When you enlarge your territory, divide the profits." He offers an early version of a corporate incentive program when he recommends rewarding a chariot to the first of a company to capture ten or more of the enemy.

Of course, the chase for money affects both sides of the lines of war. Wealth motivates the enemy as much as your own troops, so temptations of profits are a good lure to use against them. Sun Tzu advises us to "make the enemy's path circuitous and entice them with profits," implying that manipulating the opponent's greed and profit-seeking urges is the best way to throw them off track. The same holds true for higher-rank-

The Art of War

ing underlings. Sun Tzu recommends that your local feudal lords (or mid-level corporate executives) should be kept busy and distracted with a search for wealth, which will keep them out of wrangles for power: "have the feudal lords race after profits."

Sun Tzu's consistent emphasis on the importance of the financial factor of warfare gives us a glimpse of his theory of human nature. He sees all men, regardless of their rank and of what side of the battle they fight on, as alike in their underlying greed and self-interest. The wise commander will keep this in mind when dealing both with his own forces and those of the enemy.

But you need more than profit incentives to keep your people in good fighting condition. Sun Tzu recognizes the value of motivation, but he doesn't neglect an even more basic requirement: physical well-being, in the broadest sense of the term. Here again we see one of the most striking aspects of Sun Tzu's analytical genius. He grasps the most sophisticated ideas but never forgets that battles are still fought on the hard ground with people of flesh and blood. Despite his frequent flights into spirituality, he always remains attentive to the basic facts of life, to the power of hunger and fatigue as factors in military action. No matter how motivated the troops are, they can't achieve anything if they're tired and hungry. You can make strategic use of these factors not only in ensuring the material comfort of your own people, but in damaging the enemy as well: "[I]f the enemy is rested you can tire him; if he is well fed you can make him hungry." Like countless other factors, physical discomfort is a key element in the overall scheme of a battle plan.

Sun Tzu also refers to another factor in the well-being of your fighting forces, one known in Chinese culture as *qi* or *ch'i* (a different *ch'i* from the one referring to unorthodox warfare techniques, but transliterated the same way in English). We can translate this *ch'i* as "vitality" or "innermost spirit." According to the ancient Asian alternative-health practice of *reiki*, the *ch'i* can be nurtured through a careful handling of the body's energy points. It's neither completely physical nor completely mental but covers both. Sun Tzu says that if you carefully nurture your troops and don't overwork them, "their *ch'i* will be united and their strength will be at a maximum." But *ch'i* refers to more than physical well-being, for Sun Tzu refers to *ch'i* and physical strength as two different things. *Ch'i* can be dispersed or united, suggesting that it's more like inner focus than mere physical stamina.

Points of View

Nevertheless, the *ch'i* is related to the body's ups and downs, for Sun Tzu acknowledges that it changes with the body's daily cycles: "in the morning [the army's] *ch'i* is ardent; during the day their *ch'i* becomes indolent; at night their *ch'i* is exhausted." This idea of *ch'i* may be related to the feeling of intense concentration many people feel if they go to work after exercising at the gym. This vital state is the result of physical exertion but goes far beyond the body, into the realm of spiritual and mental condition. It's important to regard *ch'i* as a separate concept, something distinct from physical comfort. Doing so recognizes the crucial overflow between physical and spiritual states and underscores the need for a holistic understanding of well-being. Plans for successful warfare must take into account these holistic vitality readings of both your own troops and those of your enemy.

On the whole, Sun Tzu's ideas about what gets people motivated may come across as cynical. He appears to recognize no higher cause or sentimental drive that might spur a person to fight bravely: there is no emotional appeal to warfare for him. But we must remember that Sun Tzu lived in a radically unstable political and cultural era. We can imagine that it's hard to inspire patriotic loyalty in a population that doesn't know what new feudal warlord will claim authority over them from one day to the next.

During certain periods in Chinese history, when dynasties were more stably installed, loyalty to the leader was indeed a motivation. But in a way, the instability of Sun Tzu's environment resembles our own business climate in the U.S. Corporate regimes no longer inspire the faith or confidence they once did. Lifetime careers in a single company—or even a single industry—are increasingly rare. Workers are free agents much more so than before, with little sense of loyalty to their firms. Reading Sun Tzu reminds us that while sentimental attachments like corporate loyalty may fizzle away, worker contentment and the desire for wealth will always remain factors the wise leader can use to his advantage.

The Art of War

What does Sun Tzu recommend to a leader wishing to launch an attack? What are the general guidelines for effective attack?

KNOW WHAT YOU'RE GETTING YOURSELF INTO

Though Sun Tzu does say a good bit about defense, *The Art of War* primarily speaks about attack. In part, this slant comes from the fact that Sun Tzu participated in a number of large-scale attacks on the kingdom of Ch'u, in which aggression was essential to success. Sun Tzu's advice in this arena ranges from the practical to the metaphysical. We can benefit from this advice today if we think of "attack" in a broader sense, as any active initiative that brings us up against the obstacles standing between us and our goals. Attack isn't necessarily negative or destructive—it can be a metaphor for making progress in general.

To start off, Sun Tzu stresses the importance of knowing as much as you can about the enemy being invaded or the obstacle being tackled. It might seem like an obvious point, but Sun Tzu includes it as a warning to leaders who value intuition too much, who get swept away with hasty and ill-considered plans. We must take the necessary time to get a handle on the situation, even at critical junctures when time is in short supply. In the context of war, the commander must know the plans of local leaders in order to forge alliances before an attack on a common enemy; he must know the lay of the land he's invading in order to maneuver his resources.

Knowledge is such an intimate part of any plan for attack that Sun Tzu considers spies and reconnaissance to be crucial elements of warfare. The spy is the general's assistant: "[A]s for the armies you want to strike, the cities you want to attack, and the men you want to assassinate, you must first know the names of the defensive commander, his assistants, staff, door guards, and attendants. You must have our spies search out and learn them all." Though we may not have anything as glamorous as spies and secret agents at our disposal in the everyday world today, virtually every businessperson knows the high value of inside information in almost any situation. Today, as in ancient China, strategy is as much about information as it is about strength.

Points of View

Sun Tzu also teaches that it's impossible to mount a successful campaign unless you keep your resources unified, organized, and coherent. He compares the effective army to a Chinese snake called the *shuaijan*, which attacks with both its head and its tail—any military organization should have the same sort of organic unity.

Certain tactics encourage this kind of close-knit unification. One strategy is to push as far as possible into the enemy territory, so that your forces will be surrounded on all sides and will be held compactly as a single powerful entity. "In general," says Sun Tzu, "the Tao of an invader is that when one has penetrated deeply [into enemy territory], the army will be unified, and the defenders will not be able to conquer you." If an invasion is only shallow, and tentative, a commander must take great care to make sure the energy and organization of his forces doesn't disperse.

On the flip side, causing disunity in the enemy is equally valuable. Sun Tzu clearly advises us to "[k]eep the enemy's forward and rear forces from connecting"—his version of the familiar motto "divide and conquer." Division of the enemy is political as well as spatial. It's useful to keep their upper and lower ranks from trusting each other, to stir up antagonism between the noble and the common.

> **Today, as in ancient China, strategy is as much about information as it is about strength.**

Third, Sun Tzu urges us to be bold. This might startle us in light of Sun Tzu's constant emphasis on rational and practical preparations, on looking before we leap. But for Sun Tzu there's no contradiction between rational preparation and bold action. If we've obtained the necessary knowledge about the situation we face, we can launch our campaign boldly and decisively even into the most dangerous circumstances. Prolonged advances aren't as wise as lightning-bolt invasions: "It is the nature of the army to stress speed."

On the whole, Sun Tzu favors surprise and risk-taking—albeit well prepared and well informed risk-taking—in mounting campaigns. While a leader should always be wary of entering into absolutely desperate or

The Art of War

foolhardy situations, he shouldn't coddle the troops too much or miss any opportunities due to ignorance of the facts or fear of decisive action. Danger in battle can be an inspirational force. We might even go so far as to say that the more dangerous a situation, the more engaged a warrior's self-preservation skills will be—and the better the chances of success. In Sun Tzu's words, "Only after the masses have penetrated dangerous [terrain] will they be able to craft victory out of defeat." Sun Tzu compares an effective attack to helping your troops ascend a great height and then kicking their ladders away. Their own survival instinct will come into play, and they will fight brilliantly. In attack, after the leader ensures the unity and readiness of his troops, it's wiser for him to allow each soldier to be his own best commander than to micromanage his every move. In business management today, as on the battlefield back then, we must trust the ability of those under our command to take the most effective action: "For this reason even though the soldiers are not instructed, they are prepared; without seeking it, their cooperation is obtained."

Overall, Sun Tzu's advice on effective attack emphasizes trusting your staff and warns against excessive control over them. A good leader doesn't focus on managing his people closely in critical situations—he focuses on preparation and information-gathering so that the attack is so effective he doesn't need to manage his people closely when it's carried out. There's a surprising sense of recklessness in Sun Tzu's advice about attack—his favoring of great speed, of casting troops with decisiveness into seemingly hopeless situations. But it's not really recklessness—it's the boldness that springs from faith in the careful preparation you've done and faith in your people.

Points of View

Why does Sun Tzu focus so much on the terrain, the physical environment? Aren't the armies and leaders operating *in* the environment more important?

STOP AND LOOK AROUND YOU

Terrain doesn't just refer to the forests and the fields—it's the larger context of the battlefield's surroundings. In everyday terms we might call the terrain the whole material situation in which we are trying to achieve our goals. If Sun Tzu discussed terrain simply in the sense of the neutral backdrop to the battle, it would be uninteresting and unimportant. But there's nothing neutral about Sun Tzu's idea of terrain: for him, the landscape is virtually an active participant in the battle, just as the army and the commander are.

Sun Tzu's constant emphasis on the interrelated unity of Heaven and Earth in the Tao inextricably binds the land and the men, both in war and in other aspects of life. The land has its own vital presence, which the wise commander knows to treat with respect. Only a foolish leader would ignore the fact that where he fights matters as much as whom and how he fights. This outlook is an important difference between Sun Tzu and earlier theorists of military victory who abstractly valued Virtue and Courage above all else. Sun Tzu doesn't dismiss these lofty attributes but reminds us that we must always face reality. Our feet are always on the ground, wading through marshland or stumbling down rocky slopes. Sun Tzu's attention to the terrain is another expression of his hardheaded practical wisdom.

Some of Sun Tzu's advice might strike us as obvious. It's common sense that we should keep ourselves and those we lead out of dangerous environments—whether real, physical environments or more figurative

> ### One fatal mistake
> Napoleon was reputedly a great admirer of *The Art of War*—although his defeat at Waterloo can be seen as a huge failure to heed one of Sun Tzu's warnings about knowing the terrain.

The Art of War

ones—and beware of places rife with hiding places where our opponents might be waiting in ambush. But Sun Tzu doesn't make any claims of being brilliantly original in his instructions. *The Art of War* is a manual or handbook, and we can't expect it to omit the obvious points any more than we expect our computer instruction manual to ignore the keyboard or the on/off switch.

But Sun Tzu makes comments about the environment that are far shrewder than the obvious. Many of these comments are in specifically military terms: Sun Tzu advises not to advance toward a river that the enemy is crossing, but to wait until half the enemy forces have crossed, and then attack on dry ground. He also warns us never to face the river's current but always to keep our backs to it, as it's an obstacle to our potential escape. If we see dust rising, we should scrutinize it carefully: a narrow, rising column indicates that chariots are in motion, while a low, broad dust cloud points to advancing infantrymen.

In our context today, as in Sun Tzu's context then, all the tiny clues and details in the material surroundings, both obvious and obscure, are essential to understanding the environment in which we operate. We can't afford to neglect them. Noticing that a coworker is taking longer and longer lunch breaks may signal dissatisfaction with his job, which could be a factor in your own job advancement. Subtle cues from your manager or your employees can say volumes about their attitudes toward you and the esteem in which they hold you. Reading between the lines when observing the moves of your competitors is essential. In today's world, it's elements like these that constitute the "terrain." In a broader view, some business writers have envisioned Sun Tzu's catalog of terrains as different market situations, some more favorable than others.

During the course of *The Art of War*, Sun Tzu gives us an exhaustive survey of terrains and environments, breaking down the various kinds of landscapes into standard types, each with its own set of risks and advantages to consider. According to Sun Tzu, an "accessible" terrain is one in which both you and your opponent can advance freely, as if the field of battle were a kind of natural arena set apart from the rest of the landscape. A "stalemated" terrain offers no possibility for either you or your opponent to advance. A "suspended" configuration offers the possibility of advance but not of retreat—in which case success must be assured, for there will be no escape for the vanquished. In tight or "constricted" terrain, you

Points of View

should deploy your forces only if you arrive there before the enemy does; if the enemy is already present, you should depart immediately.

Sun Tzu concludes his catalog with a discussion of "expansive" or spread-out terrain. In this kind of environment, no special arena for fighting can be located—it's the middle of nowhere. Sun Tzu views expansive terrains as the worst setting for battle: "[E]ngaging in combat will not be advantageous." This assertion might strike us as odd, for we may imagine that an open, expansive plain would be the best possible place for confrontation. But we must remember that for Sun Tzu, the terrain isn't just a place but a *participant* in the battle. In that light, a wide-open terrain with no distinguishing features offers no natural features to use to your advantage. Whenever we are about to act, we must locate where we are in the catalog of fighting environments.

Sun Tzu goes so far in emphasizing the lay of the land that he sets up a step-by-step progression from knowledge of the terrain to victory. At the end of the fourth section of *The Art of War*, he says that, first of all, terrain gives birth to measurement, as men assess the distance from their sheltering hills to the open plains of battle and so on. Second, measurement gives rise to an estimation of forces—large or small forces, as the size of the venue dictates—which in turn leads to calculation of the number of men required for a given maneuver. Third, knowing manpower requirements allows us to weigh strength. And finally, weighing strength, according to Sun Tzu, "gives birth to victory." According to this progression toward victory, the first step of familiarity with the terrain isn't simply advisable but apparently necessary—just as one needs to step on the first rung when climbing up a ladder, there's no way for an astute commander to bypass intimate knowledge of the landscape. In Sun Tzu's description, it's like a law of nature that victory will issue from knowing the terrain: he says that A "gives birth" to B, and B to C, as if speaking of natural reproduction. If a leader gives the terrain appropriate attention, his success will come just as surely as the cycles of nature.

The emphasis on the terrain and environment embodies Sun Tzu's respect for the powers that be. Nature is unrelenting and unstoppable. For Sun Tzu, it symbolizes everything that must be what it is and must do what it does. In conflicts, we should embrace this power. Just as the origins of success are entwined with the landscape, so too is the final victory, which Sun Tzu sometimes describes as a natural inevitability like the flow of a river.

The Art of War

In one of the poetic touches sprinkled throughout *The Art of War*, Sun Tzu concludes his summation on terrain and victory with a comparison of the triumphant army to nothing other than a part of the landscape, a waterfall: "The combat of the victorious is like the sudden release of a pent-up torrent down a thousand-fathom gorge." This image is only a simile, and Sun Tzu may only choose the waterfall because of its immense and unstoppable force. But by evoking a natural image of the terrain here, he also cleverly hints at how natural and inevitable it can be to attain success if the environment is taken into consideration. After all, a waterfall doesn't have to strive or *try* to release its torrents down the gorge—the release happens naturally. In the same way, Sun Tzu hints that a wise commander in touch with his natural surroundings and material circumstances will ultimately achieve victory.

○ ○ ○

Sun Tzu places a strong emphasis on the concepts of *ch'i* and *cheng*, or unorthodox and orthodox techniques. What does he mean by these? Why are they so important?

MIX IT UP A LITTLE

Sun Tzu balances a respect for proper procedure with a zeal for creative thinking. Everything depends on maintaining that balance in our actions. Traditional Chinese thought has always shown a fondness for conceptual pairs held in balance—*yin* and *yang* being the most famous example. Indeed, Sun Tzu refers to *yin* and *yang* several times in his work.

But more crucial is the *ch'i* (unorthodox) and *cheng* (orthodox) pairing in the fifth section of *The Art of War*. We might paraphrase them in more standard English by seeing *cheng* as playing by the book, following the rules, and *ch'i* as being spontaneous and unpredictable, letting creativity take the lead. Sun Tzu begins the important fifth section of his work by saying that these two concepts, presumably more than anything

Points of View

else, are what enable armies to "withstand the enemy without being defeated." Since Sun Tzu doesn't privilege one more than the other with regard to warfare, we see that both *ch'i* and *cheng* are equally valuable to a wise strategist.

Orthodox and unorthodox are both significant, and they're inextricably bound to each other. Sun Tzu says, "the changes of the unorthodox and the orthodox can never be completely exhausted. The unorthodox and orthodox mutually produce each other, just like an endless cycle. Who can exhaust them?" We may never be able to call one more important than the other, but our task as leaders is to determine when one should be used and the other suspended. There's nothing easy about this task, for there's no rule about when to use rules and when to refrain from them. We need an instinct for it.

Balancing the orthodox and the unorthodox is an art, not a science. Sun Tzu hints at this idea when he compares the two all-encompassing terms to the scale of notes in music and to the palette of colors: "The notes do not exceed five, but the changes of the five notes can never be fully heard. The colors do not exceed five, but the changes of the five colors can never be completely seen." Managing this delicate artistic balance requires a fullness of spirit that goes far beyond a calculating mind.

> **Sun Tzu favors creative, spontaneous solutions as much as textbook solutions.**

It's interesting that Sun Tzu favors creative, spontaneous solutions as much as textbook solutions, especially because *The Art of War* is a textbook or manual, and like all manuals it claims to give certain rules to guide us. But by stressing the equal importance of both *ch'i* and *cheng*, Sun Tzu effectively says that no manual can claim to teach us all we need to know. Rules are crucial and indispensable but only go so far in determining effective action.

Here we see why Sun Tzu is known as a philosopher or sage—"Master Sun"—rather than a mere technician of military strategy. Like other great sages such as Buddha and Jesus, Sun Tzu recognizes the limits of rational thinking and rules, and pays tribute to the fundamental mystery and irra-

29

tionality of life's activities. In the passage that praises the unorthodox or *ch'i* modes of warfare, Sun Tzu sounds like a poet or prophet much more than a technical writer: "Thus one who excels at sending forth the unorthodox is as inexhaustible as Heaven, as unlimited as the Yangtze and Yellow rivers. What reach an end and begin again are the sun and moon. What die and are reborn are the four seasons." We must be poets as well as logicians in leadership positions. Man-made rules are useful, but natural strokes of genius are as sublime as rivers, heavens, seasons, and celestial bodies. Rules are constant, whereas strokes of genius are harder to control or retain, reaching an end and beginning again whether we like it or not.

The nearest Sun Tzu comes to defining the proper roles of the orthodox and unorthodox is his brief assertion that they may be used at different stages: the orthodox gets the ball rolling, while the unorthodox is brought in later to finish things off. Sun Tzu sees orthodox or *cheng* strategies as a means of initiating a conflict, whereas he sees unorthodox or *ch'i* strokes of genius as a way to carry it to its triumphant conclusion. "In general," he writes, "in battle one engages with the orthodox and gains victory through the unorthodox." Translated into our more colloquial terms, he means that the rules of the game are best observed at the outset of any encounter with an opponent, but then should be supplemented with the unpredictable moves that win the prize. Sun Tzu doesn't explain explicitly why rules are best used early on. However, we could surmise that a sudden shift from playing by the book to flouting all rules is a highly effective way of throwing off the enemy. They'll assume they grasp the way things are going, only to be startled by a sudden twist of maneuver for which they're unprepared.

What's crucial about Sun Tzu's *ch'i / cheng* pairing is that it's definitely *not* a good-versus-bad value opposition. One isn't better than the other. Nor should a wise leader embrace one while rejecting the other. If we read *The Art of War* too quickly or carelessly, we may come away with a mistaken impression that Sun Tzu values creative and spontaneous thinking at *all* times, and that for him the ideal general—or in modern terms, the business leader—is a kind of freethinking, intuitive, artistic type. This is not true. Sun Tzu does use artistic metaphors in his discussion of strategy, but the art for him lies not in a full-scale barrage of creativity but rather in the harmonious orchestration of the orthodox and unorthodox notes—a complex choreography of the planned and the

Points of View

spontaneous, the rational and the off-the-cuff. The truly successful leader is the one who knows intuitively when to set aside intuition and play by the book for a while—and vice versa.

○ ○ ○

Why does Sun Tzu value deception so highly? Why does he appear to downplay the hard facts of reality in favor of illusion?

A LITTLE DISINFORMATION GOES A LONG WAY

To Sun Tzu, trickery is key. He places an extraordinary amount of emphasis on the ability to deceive one's opponent, even going so far as to call it the very essence of battle: "Warfare is the Way (Tao) of deception." This is an extreme statement. In short, Sun Tzu implies that in waging war we're not on the path of aggression, survival, or any other active concept we might associate with fighting—but rather on the path of falsehood. Deception is not simply *one* of the Ways of war: there is only one way or Tao, and deception is it; there is no way to avoid it. Sun Tzu's assertion is startling, and it has drawn much attention from commentators over the centuries. Yet what Sun Tzu means by deception is subtle. Some readers oversimplify this point, regarding Sun Tzu as little more than a prophet of hoodwinking, a master of illusion. According to this view, Sun Tzu's art of war is like running a particularly elaborate and dangerous funhouse hall of mirrors in which to confuse and trap your enemy. But this is unfair.

Sun Tzu emphasizes the power of illusion, perhaps partly as a rhetorical effect to make us sit up and take notice, but he in no way undermines the importance of the solid reality behind illusion. As with every point in *The Art of War*—and many points in Chinese philosophy as a whole—deception is closely tied up with its opposite, straightforwardness or truth. Like *yin* and *yang*, or Sun Tzu's favorite pair *ch'i* and *cheng*, successful battle involves a delicate interplay between illusion and reality. It requires a commander who knows how to balance the two effectively.

The Art of War

The examples Sun Tzu uses illustrate this need for balance. He advises, "Thus, although [you are] capable, display incapability to them. When committed to employing your forces, feign inactivity. When [your objective] is nearby, make it appear as if distant; when far away, create the illusion of being nearby." The reality of capability is just as key as the illusion of incapability, just as the truth of an objective being nearby is just as essential as creating the appearance that it is far away. If Sun Tzu were only a trickster who sees warfare as a vast sleight-of-hand performance, then he would simply focus on the display and ignore the reality—but he doesn't. A mere illusion of incapability would serve nothing if there were not real capability on hand. The illusion only works if the contrary reality looms behind it. The two work in tandem.

> **Moderation is key in handing out both rewards and punishments.**

Moreover, we can't assume that deceit refers to one thing only. For Sun Tzu, deception covers a wide array of tactics and deployments that run the spectrum from passive misleading to active deception and manipulation. A passive deception would be allowing a false belief to arise in the mind of the enemy by shielding them from the truth. For example, the enemy's belief that you are inactive when in fact you're busily preparing for attack would be a passive kind of illusion—you're withholding the truth, passively allowing the enemy to come to their wrong-headed conclusions. But other strategies clearly involve more active, interfering forms of artifice. Sun Tzu's advice that we "be deferential to foster their arrogance" refers to a more aggressive kind of mind-control in which we actively manipulate the opponent's behavior, not just their beliefs. Flattery makes the enemy haughty and therefore overly self-confident and unsuspecting of our insidious plans to undo him.

For Sun Tzu, deception can involve some lofty mind games. At one point he refers to knowing how to manipulate what he calls "the formless," which we could define as everything not quite graspable by the senses and mind. This manipulation of the formless is unlike regular deception: rather than replace a fact with a falsehood in the enemy's mind, you replace a fact with nothing at all—a blurry shape where an

Points of View

idea should be. The formless refers to the dark and hazy background to our well-lit ideas and concepts. It's not just a passive fact of life but a powerful resource to use against the enemy. Sun Tzu becomes lyrical when praising the deceptive powers of the formless: "Thus when someone excels in attacking, the enemy does not know where to mount his defense; when someone excels at defense, the enemy does not know where to attack. Subtle! Subtle! It approaches the formless. Spiritual! Spiritual! It attains the soundless. Thus he can become the enemy's Master of Fate."

Sun Tzu's Zen-like exclamations about the spiritual wonders of the formless may seem exaggerated, but the formless is the key to his whole philosophy. The art of warfare involves much more than taking effective action, which, though indispensable, isn't everything. Effective action involves only what exists and what occurs. True warfare also involves what is *not* there and what does *not* occur. For Sun Tzu, the glass is always both half full *and* half empty, and the battlefield is the same. The half-empty aspect might be precisely what overcomes your enemy. Knowing when to make use of the nonexistent is the highest form of deception and a true spiritual achievement.

○ ○ ○

How should a leader use rewards and punishments for optimum effect?

DOLE THEM OUT—BUT WISELY

Sun Tzu sees rewards and punishments as ways to remind people of the importance of the organization to which they belong, be it an army, a company, or simply a project team. If someone in the group goes wrong, the leader punishes that person on the basis of group identity, not on the basis of individual acts. Without a sense of such an organization, the troops will perceive punishments as scattershot or arbitrary and will sorely resent them: "If you impose punishments on the troops before they have become attached, they will not be submissive. If they are not submissive, they will be difficult to employ."

The Art of War

The flip side of this guideline is that an organization without any imposed punishments will be dysfunctional. Keeping the troops functioning well requires some display of strictness: "If you do not impose punishments after the troops have become attached, they cannot be used." Here, Sun Tzu suggests that there's a close relationship between corporate or communal identity on one hand and an awareness of a system of punishments on the other. Punishment thus not only deters wrongdoing but also helps to forge a solid sense of group identity.

As far as rewards are concerned, Sun Tzu is an unabashed materialist with little interest in symbolic rewards. Cash means far more to him than pats on the back or honorary commendations. The commemorative plaque at a company retirement party is meaningless compared to a big fat check. When financial rewards are materially sufficient, they can be very valuable as powerful incentives to effective behavior: "Thus in chariot encounters, when ten or more chariots are captured, reward the first to get one." The idea of an employee incentive program, which Sun Tzu described 2,500 years ago, is still recognized as a good way to give workers individual initiative that will bring good to the larger group.

Significantly, Sun Tzu makes no place for stinginess in his theory of rewards. The bigger the victory, the greater the profit sharing: "When you plunder a district, divide the wealth among your troops. When you enlarge your territory, divide the profits." It's striking that Sun Tzu doesn't recommend dividing the wealth among the ranking officers only. He writes that it should be shared among all the troops, in a democratic show of corporate equality that ensures loyalty and staves off mutiny.

In short, moderation is key in handing out both rewards and punishments. According to Sun Tzu, too much of either one spells trouble: "One who frequently grants rewards is in deep distress. One who frequently imposes punishments is in great difficulty." With his characteristic style, Sun Tzu doesn't explain *why* excessive rewards and punishments suggest difficulty and distress. It may be that too many rewards spoil the troops or encourage competition among them, or that too many punishments ruin morale. But Sun Tzu suggests that punishments and rewards are an index of leadership skills, not of troop performance.

Sun Tzu considers the overload of punishments and rewards as a sign of problems in the commander, not in the troops. He doesn't even entertain the thought that a much-punished detachment of soldiers is perform-

Points of View

ing poorly and that they might actually deserve all that punishment. The troops have very little to do with the issue. Sun Tzu's focus on the punisher rather than those who are punished shows us that overdone punishments and rewards are symptoms of leadership problems—not the *cause* of these problems. When we see a commander being too harsh, we can guess that he's making a desperate attempt to bring order to his ranks. We can read the symptoms of poor leadership in that commander just as a doctor reads the signs of a patient's illness. A leader should thus be wary of excesses in meting out justice, for excessive punishing or rewarding could signal that he's losing grip on his command.

All these points underscore the most striking aspect of Sun Tzu's view of rewards and punishments: they aren't correlated with moral behavior. Sun Tzu lets us know that punishment is crucially important but doesn't fill us in on *what* should be punished. He doesn't spell out any code of conduct that the reward and punishment system would enforce. He doesn't say, for example, that loyalty to the commander is the highest good and therefore disloyalty should be punished most severely. Is treason always more punishable than insubordination? If troops disobey but do so in a way that leads to victory, should the troops be rewarded or punished?

Sun Tzu leaves such questions unanswered, as if they're irrelevant to his vision of warfare. His silence on the specifics of punishments and rewards might just be another example of his silence on moral matters altogether. Just as he never talks about the ethics of battle, the difference between just and unjust wartime killing, or any moral dimension to warfare at all, so too does he keep quiet about the ethical rights and wrongs that merit rewards and punishments. But we must keep in mind that Sun Tzu is writing a technical guide to effective leadership, not to the ethics of war. He only answers how-to questions rather than probe moral justice.

Sun Tzu's dismissal of ethics in questions of punishment makes us think about the value of punitive action. It draws our attention to its practical effects and the ways a savvy leader can use punishment as a creative tool. When Sun Tzu urges us to "bestow rewards not required by law," we realize again that he prefers to envision rewards and punishments not as mechanical formulas but as instruments by which the smart leader can carve out his own center of power above those he leads. The leader should distribute punishments and rewards automatically, like frequent flyer miles—but should dole them out with a little street-smart creativity as well.

The Art of War

Why does Sun Tzu endorse espionage so warmly? Doesn't his enthusiasm for the underhanded use of spies contradict his lofty spiritual message?

DON'T BE AFRAID TO GET YOUR HANDS DIRTY

Though Sun Tzu is spiritual, his spirituality is realistic. As we see time and again, he worships the idea of effectiveness: he pays close attention to the nitty-gritty details of the world around him and to knowing how to manipulate them. He's not simply an introspective searcher. The popular view that Sun Tzu's ideal commander is like Obi-Wan Kenobi in *Star Wars*—a transcendent individual disdaining material things as interfering with his pure inner search—is a major misconception.

Sun Tzu was a tough and detail-minded realist as well as a lofty philosopher. He rejected the old noble Chinese faith in virtue as the guiding light for leaders. He refused to advise a Zen withdrawal from messy situations, counseling instead a firm-fisted grappling with them. He always grounds the spiritual dimension of *The Art of War* in practices that efficiently achieve the desired result. Espionage is a perfect case in point. While Sun Tzu certainly values the inward harmony of the individual leader, he values with equal enthusiasm cruder aspects of leadership, such as the hiring of spies. His survey of the various types of spies is exhaustive, and we can sense his approval of espionage in the detailed precision he brings to the subject.

There are five main types of spies: local spies drawn from the population nearby, internal spies who hold government positions, double agents employed by the enemy, expendable spies who spread disinformation outside the kingdom, and living spies who return from abroad with their reports. Each of these types fulfills its own vital function in warfare, and together they represent the single most effective tool available to the ruler. Sun Tzu is unwavering in his praise of the value of spies: "Thus of all the Three Armies' affairs no relationship is closer than with spies; no rewards are more generous than those given to spies, no affairs more secret than those pertaining to spies." The ethical objection to the use of spies carries absolutely no weight at all for Sun Tzu. He simply doesn't mention it.

Points of View

The ever-practical Sun Tzu also praises the use of spies on financial grounds, as a money-saving strategy. He points out the absurdity of a commander who launches an army of a hundred thousand men—spending a thousand pieces of gold per day and putting seven hundred thousand families out of work—and then remains locked in a standoff for years. If the commander just spent a hundred pieces of gold on a spy's services, chances are he could obtain a quick victory. Sun Tzu is fierce in his scorn of this type of leader, calling his behavior "the ultimate inhumanity" and asserting that he "is not a general for the people . . . or the arbiter of victory." The failure to use spies simply isn't cost-effective, though spies might seem pricey at first. Even the especially high rewards given to double agents are worth it in the long run. In Sun Tzu's words, "enlightened rulers and sagacious generals who are able to get intelligent spies will invariably attain great achievements."

Sun Tzu also has no patience for commanders who place a mystical faith in occult signs and spirits. He sees nothing otherworldly about the knowledge that must be obtained to ensure victory: it's worldly knowledge about men that "cannot be gained from ghosts and spirits . . . but must be gained from men for it is the knowledge of the enemy's true situation." Sun Tzu backs up his point with a couple of august examples of spies from Chinese history: I Chih, who was a Yin spy among the Hsia, and later Lü Ya, who was a Chou spy among the Yin. "This is the essence of the military," Sun Tzu says. He looks at the success of the spies from a purely analytical perspective, one immune to any patriotic support or disapproval of either of these two spies' dynasties. Sun Tzu's faith in spies thus underscores the commonsensical—but easily overlooked—fact that victory isn't fated or predestined by heaven, but is in the hands of leaders who patiently gather and analyze information.

The commander's role in the institution of espionage is not passive. He doesn't simply wait around for the spies to return with their reports. On the contrary, the use of spies demands the most active application of a leader's intelligence. A spy's report is more than a set of facts. It's a text to be carefully examined for inconsistencies and falsehoods, because a leader can never know for sure when his man may have turned against him.

Sun Tzu does make some comments on espionage that border on the moral and ethical. Spies may be useful, but only for the enlightened and wise commander: "Unless someone has the wisdom of a Sage, he cannot use spies; unless he is benevolent and righteous, he cannot employ spies; unless he is subtle and perspicacious, he cannot perceive the substance in intelligence reports." He implies that the commander's ability to use espionage to his advantage is a measure of his overall leadership skills. He must be practical rather than bold, valuing the quiet gathering of information over the flashy deployment of troops. He must have the fiscal wisdom to realize that substantial spending on spies will be easily recouped in the long run. And finally, the leader must have the expert familiarity with human nature to sense disloyalty among his spies, to know how to read between the lines of intelligence reports. In short, a good leader, then, is a good employer of spies.

A WRITER'S LIFE

The Man Behind the Myth

Sun Tzu himself remains shrouded in mystery, with some historians going so far as to question whether he existed at all.

○ ○ ○

SUN TZU'S NAME IS WIDELY KNOWN, but his biography remains murky and uncertain. Historians in China and abroad have traditionally identified him as a military leader and tactician originally named Sun Wu, who was active around 510 or 512 B.C. His exploits are recorded in the chronicles called *The Spring and Autumn Annals of Wu and Yüeh* and the *Shih chi*. According to those works, Sun Wu fought heroically in the wars between the Chinese kingdoms of Wu, Chu'u, and Yüeh.

A gifted strategist and commander, Sun Wu was glorified enough to receive the honorable title *tzu* (or *zi* in the more modern transcription system) meaning "master" or "sage," which was also bestowed upon the great philosophers Confucius ("Kung-zi," or Master Kung in Chinese) and Mencius ("Meng-zi," Master Meng). Sun Wu thus is enshrined in Chinese tradition as much more than a general of great talent—he's regarded as a philosopher, a wise man of the battlefield.

Of course we should beware of confusing fact and fiction and shouldn't take the content of these ancient chronicles as necessarily accurate. In Sun Tzu's case, though, fiction and myth are almost all we have beyond a tiny skeleton of historical data. He has huge importance in Chinese culture, but isn't associated with the countless anecdotes and lesson tales that other Chinese sages attracted over time. Children aren't told traditional stories about Sun Tzu as they're told about Confucius, Mencius, and others. The question why is only one of many mysteries about Sun Tzu's life and career.

The Art of War

The chronicle *The Spring and Autumn Annals of Wu and Yüeh* records that Sun Wu was a native of the kingdom of Wu, that he was known for his skills at formulating military strategy, and that he preferred to live apart from men, keeping his gifts a secret. But Sun Wu was known to the king of Wu's capable minister, Wu Tzu-hsü, who mentioned Sun Wu's name seven times during a conference with the king of Wu. The king summoned Sun Wu to court and questioned the mysterious master on tactical matters. When Sun Wu answered all the questions with intelligence and insight, the king was pleased and proposed a small test of Sun Wu's military organization skills. Sun Wu agreed and suggested that he be made a makeshift commander of an army composed of the king's 300 female concubines. The two favorite royal concubines would be named lieutenants, each in command of a company. The startled king gave his consent and ordered his concubines to be outfitted with helmets and armor, swords, and shields. Sun Wu proceeded to give this female army orders: on the first drum beat the women were to assemble, on the second they were to advance, and on the third they were to deploy into military formations. But when the drum beat, the women only covered their mouths and giggled. Sun Wu reportedly took the drums himself and beat them three times, explaining the orders five times. Yet still the women could only laugh hysterically.

Sun Wu's reaction to his concubine army's incessant giggling was stormy and unforgiving. The *Shih chi* records that his hair stood on end under his cap, his eyes opened wide, and he roared in rage "like a terrifying tiger." He announced that it's the general's fault when his orders are vague and unclear, but that his own orders were repeated three times and explained five times. Concluding that he himself wasn't being vague, the fault, therefore, must lie with the army.

Sun Wu asked the Master of Laws what the traditional punishment for military insubordination was. When the Master answered that it was decapitation, Sun Wu ordered the executioner's axes brought forward and commanded the decapitation of the army's two lieutenants—the king's favorite concubines. Just when the execution was about to be carried out, the king happened to mount his observation platform and saw what was underway. He ordered a messenger to rush to the field with a stay of execution, saying that the king recognized Sun Wu's abilities in commanding an army, but that if the two royal favorites were killed, the

A Writer's Life

king's food would no longer be sweet. Astonishingly, Sun Wu sent word back to the king that, as he understood traditional military protocol, once a ruler instates a general, the general has no obligation to obey that ruler's orders regarding military matters. Sun Wu proceeded with the decapitation of the two favorite concubines.

After the execution, the army was, not surprisingly, much more obedient. When Sun Wu beat his drum, they silently fell into place according to the prescribed military etiquette. The women warriors didn't even dare to make eye contact with one another. Sun Wu announced to the king that his army was well prepared for fighting, able to withstand fire and water without any difficulty, and able to accomplish any feat under heaven.

The king was reportedly displeased, telling Sun Wu that while it was obvious he was a talented commander, there was no place to exercise such an army. Sun Wu's display of organizational prowess had gone too far, and the king told the general to go home immediately. At this point, the king's minister Wu Tzu-hsü spoke up, saying that the formation of an army was a serious matter of great auspiciousness, meaning—according to traditional Chinese thought—that it was of deep heavenly significance. The minister said that if an army were formed but then never used for an attack—and, at the time, an attack of that very kind was then required against the enemy state of Ch'u—then the military Tao or heavenly way would be violated. Wu Tzu-hsü urged the king to grant Sun Wu full authority to lead the new army against Ch'u. The king assented, and Ch'u was attacked.

This tale of Sun Wu and the concubine army may well be purely myth and legend. But it clearly etches a legendary image of Sun Wu's iron will, adherence to the job at hand, and courage even before kings. A general who could build a fighting machine from luxury-spoiled royal concubines deserves the renown his name has gathered through the ages.

Aside from *The Spring and Autumn Annals*, the other main source of historical information on Sun Tzu is another text, the *Shih chi*. This second source asserts that Sun Tzu hailed not from Wu but from the state of Ch'i. This story implies a different cultural background: Ch'i was on the outskirts of the territories of the ruling Chou dynasty and was known for its mix of traditions and schools of thought—the sort of environment favorable for the development of a freethinking genius like Sun Tzu, unconstrained by stifling conventions.

The Art of War

The idea that Sun Tzu might be from the state of Ch'i implies that he was familiar with the thought of an earlier theorist of war named T'ai Kung, who was known in Ch'i but relatively unknown in Wu. If Sun Tzu was from Ch'i, he was probably also familiar with the Chinese military classic called *The Six Secret Teachings* (though there's some doubt as to whether that work was composed before or after *The Art of War*).

The *Shih chi* confirms one tale recorded in *The Spring and Autumn Annals*—that Sun Tzu led a campaign against the state of Ch'u in 511 B.C. The *Shih chi* adds to the story, telling that Sun Tzu moved onward into the states Ch'i and Chin, making his name known to all the local feudal lords on the way. If Sun Tzu hailed from Ch'i, as the *Shih chi* asserts, then Sun Tzu would've been instrumental in conquering his home state, as the king of Wu emerged as vanquisher of Ch'i by virtue of Sun Tzu's command.

In a fascinating turn, Sun Tzu disappeared from historical view at the peak of his military success. His name is never mentioned again. Rival theories assert that the new king executed Sun Tzu after he became dangerously embroiled in court politics, or that Sun Tzu simply acknowledged the hardships of staying afloat politically in uncertain times and willingly retired. Traditional Chinese lore lovingly embraces the latter theory, probably because it gives Sun Tzu credit for taking his fate into his own hands, for achieving the noble act of renouncing power at the apex of his career.

This legend of Sun Tzu's retirement likely gained credence because of the earlier, historically verified case of Fan Li, a Yüeh commander who conquered the state of Wu and then sailed off to sea, never to be heard from again. Indeed, a bestselling novel about Sun Tzu called the *Tung-chou lieh-kuo-chih* (written much later, during the Ming dynasty of 1368–1644 A.D.), gives a nearly Hollywood-style glamour to Sun Tzu's retirement from the world of politics and war. According to the novel's historical fiction, King Wu's minister tried to keep Sun Wu from retiring by offering him a cushy official position. When Sun Wu declined the offer and persisted in his wish to go live in the mountains, the king had his minister detain the general. Boldly, Sun Wu asked the royal minister whether he knew the Tao of Heaven, which asserts that after summer goes, winter arrives. In the same way, said Sun Wu, any attempt to rest comfortably on his present successes would inevitably lead to later mis-

A Writer's Life

fortunes—so he deemed it best to beat fate and retire immediately. This philosophical answer allegedly persuaded the minister and king to let Sun Wu go. As parting gifts, they presented Sun Wu with carriages laden with gold and silk, which the retiring general distributed to the poor on his way out of the state capital. Like the historical sources, The Ming novel declares, "no one knew how he ended up."

In the end, Sun Tzu remains a great historical mystery. Some scholars surmise that so little is remembered about him because he was overshadowed by the larger-than-life career of King Wu's minister, Wu Tzu-hsü. By this theory, the minister provided so many lively tales of adventure and soap-opera betrayal that it was never necessary to glamorize the more practical figure of Sun Tzu.

Other historians go further, doubting that we can consider Sun Tzu the author of *The Art of War* in the first place. Though they concede the historical existence and military activity of the man Sun Wu, they note anachronisms in *The Art of War* that suggest a later authorship that was artificially backdated to the sixth century B.C., perhaps in order to enhance the prestige of the work by ascribing it to a past hero. These historians also point out that the fullest record of the era's historical and political events, a chronicle entitled the *Tso chuan*, fails to mention any Sun Wu. They also note that the intricate large-scale maneuvers described in *The Art of War* weren't typical of the cruder and smaller battles of the period. While the manual asserts that the siege of a city requires many months, historical evidence shows that cities were too small in Sun Tzu's day to be besieged at all.

Finally, certain extremist historians even doubt whether Sun Wu existed at all. One theory asserts that the minister Wu Tzu-hsü and Sun Tzu were the same man, that Wu Tzu-hsü wrote the book that he nicknamed Sun in deference to the military lore passed down through the Sun family. Since Wu Tzu-hsü's son apparently later took the Sun name as his own, this theory does have some credibility. But most scholars still accept the view that a gifted general and strategist named Sun Wu—glorified later as Sun Tzu or "Master Sun"—was active around 512 B.C. and penned the work we know as *The Art of War*.

THE WORLD OUTSIDE

Dawning of a New Age

China in Sun Tzu's time was in the midst of sweeping change, as ancient traditions fell victim to a new push toward practicality.

○ ○ ○

SUN TZU LIVED DURING A TIME in Chinese history often referred to as the Spring and Autumn period, after a famous literary classic that narrated its events. The period was characterized by widespread political instability and confusion. The Chou dynasty, which had risen to power over the Shang in 1045 B.C., no longer prevailed as an unquestionable authority in the land. Weakened by ill-advised forays into the south, the overextended Chou empire was beset by barbarian attacks from the north and west. Chou leaders, once famed for their strength and resolve, had become weak and corrupted by luxury. In 770 B.C., a Chou king was forced to commit the humiliating act of transferring his capital eastward to escape barbarians to the west. While later Chou kings maintained the fiction that their dynasty continued as late as 256 B.C., their rule was fragile at best.

As Chou power diminished, various factions stepped in to assert their might. Feudal lords who once paid tribute to the Chou ruler now scrambled for ascendancy. In many states within the dissolving empire, the families of high-powered ministers took over control of the government from the rightful ruling families. Many noble families were lowered to the status of commoners while their former employees held sway above them. Long-established social hierarchies crumbled. Many land workers became tenants of their land, no longer symbolic possessions of a king but rather free agents looking after their own best interests.

The Art of War

> **Going out on top**
> Chinese tradition holds that Sun Tzu willingly disappeared from public view at the height of his powers, after his successful conquest of the kingdom of Ch'u.

The chaos that reigned over many parts of China at this time led to vast shifts in popular attitudes toward power, tradition, and authority. Ancient notions of chivalry in warfare that had been passed down for centuries as part of the Chinese cultural legacy began to lose some of their luster. After all, mercenaries and conscripted soldiers—who were becoming more numerous in the standing armies of the day—fought for pay, not honor. Originally, battles and warfare were governed by rules of etiquette that respected the *li* or "forms of appropriateness" advanced by Chinese thinkers as the highest standards of behavior in all aspects of life. But as the strife of the Spring and Autumn period increased, military leaders saw the *li* as a hindrance to efficient fighting and gradually abandoned them.

China in Sun Tzu's time was moving away from formal and symbolic obligations that had once upheld society and toward a more practical and individualistic power structure. People at all levels of society, from kings to farmers, no longer felt honor-bound to go through symbolic motions of loyalty—instead, they began to take care of themselves. For better or worse, enterprise became less state-based, more locally focused. Whereas in the Chou dynasty it would've been important for a minor landowner to curry favor with his overlord, in Sun Tzu's time it was more of a priority for the landlord to think rationally and strategically about his well-being and take accountability for his own successes. Clear-headedness became more important than flattery. We can see the new emphasis on practicality emerging in this difficult but enlightening period of Chinese history throughout *The Art of War*.

The market for practical wisdom about warfare—and other aspects of life—arose as a new phenomenon in Chinese history. Much like medieval Europe before the hardheaded Machiavelli revolutionized its ideas of power, China in earlier dynasties had tended to dismiss the practical details of statecraft in favor of soft, abstract ideas of glory and virtue. Lead-

The World Outside

ers weren't expected to dirty their hands with lowly issues of warfare, for leadership was seen as a pure, lofty, and symbolic function.

This pure view of leadership drew on the spiritual bent of Chinese culture that would later find expression in Confucianism. In the earlier dynasties (and later ones too), it was bolstered by a form of patriotism that saw China so clearly as the unquestionable exemplar of grandeur and civilization that it would be inconceivable to imagine a foreign power taking control. The greatness of China would always prevail, so petty thoughts of defense were largely unnecessary.

In some respects, a seemingly complacent attitude was valid. Invaders like the barbarian Chou gradually became just as Chinese as those they vanquished, so China always did prevail in the end. But in the Spring and Autumn period, the enemy was no longer invading barbarians but rather the Chinese themselves, drawn into internal strife. The old myth of China's grandeur became harder to celebrate as the Chinese factions multiplied and fought among themselves. In large part, Sun Tzu's achievement was to revise the spiritual legacy that defined China's past greatness—to yoke it into a hardheaded practicality that viewed statecraft as a hands-on business.

The chief conflict of the period in which Sun Tzu lived was between the established state of Ch'u and the upwardly mobile state of Wu to the east. Ch'u enjoyed the advantage of larger armies, but its tactical style was crude, neglecting the possibilities of the infantry and navy. Ch'u had long been trying to dominate Wu, but its attempts appear to have been ineffective and disorganized. The numerous ponds and marshes of Wu, in sharp contrast to the flat, dry plains of Ch'u, proved difficult for the chariots that made up the bulk of the Ch'u military forces. The Ch'u invaders seemed unable to devise more efficient methods of attack. Ch'u ended up dissipating its resources in the long attempt to dominate Wu— a prime example bearing out Sun Tzu's stringent warning against prolonged sieges.

The Ch'u government made many mistakes. With drawn-out campaigns, manpower for the battlefield was increasingly resistant or not forthcoming, and heavy war taxes depleted the economy. Ch'u leaders had extravagant tastes, imitating the last king of the Shang dynasty in spending vast sums on pleasure palaces that removed the workforce from the fields during crucial harvest times. They lacked a clear idea of their

The Art of War

aims in engaging the Wu in battle and in pursuing a larger vision for their kingdom overall. Moreover, the state of Ch'u followed a policy of bitterly repressing the smaller fiefdoms and minority groups within it. This oppression made it harder to count on the minority groups' support in warfare. The kingdom of Wu later used these minority groups' hatred of Ch'u to its own advantage.

A large-scale Ch'u foray into Wu territory in 538 B.C. met with failure, as the Ch'u forces found the Wu army prepared and well armed. This retreat heralds the end of Ch'u domination and sets the stage for Sun Tzu's glorious conquest of Ch'u and its capital city a quarter century later. As time went on, the state of Wu began to make more aggressive moves against the cities of Ch'u, which in 538 B.C. initiated large-scale defense-building projects, including the construction of heavily walled cities.

The time of open, heated conflict between the two states had dawned. Historians note several reasons for Wu's rising prospects in this conflict. Wu differed from Ch'u in its forceful and visionary leadership, strongly unified and goal-oriented. Because the vast Ch'u forces so outnumbered Wu's smaller army, strategy became more important than blunt manpower as a path to victory. Wu was much quicker than Ch'u to accept talented officers and advisors, allowing them to rise in their careers with little regard for their social origins or their support within high circles of influence. The use of trickery, ruses, and the accelerated movement of troops were characteristics of Wu warfare even before Sun Tzu arrived on the scene. He was a brilliant consolidator of Wu military technique, which is an indispensable background to *The Art of War*.

The mounting tensions between the weakening Ch'u and the strengthening Wu led to the great battle of Chi-fu in 519 B.C. Despite superior numbers, the Ch'u forces were solidly defeated. The fact that Chi-fu lay well within Ch'u borders made their losses shameful and symbolic—the end of Ch'u was at hand. This underdog victory by the smaller Wu forces is a fitting emblem of the spirit of *The Art of War*, which repeatedly discounts the importance of larger armies, and values tactics and planning instead.

Wu commanders used the tricks and deceptions in the battle of Chi-fu that Sun Tzu later advocated in his manual, leading the enemy into confusion that weakened their organization. The Wu leaders focused their attention on the armies of the border peoples on the margins of

The World Outside

Ch'u territories, who both hated Ch'u and foresaw that Ch'u could hardly protect them anymore. These smaller armies gradually joined the Wu forces as allies. The outcome of the battle only hastened the dissolution of Ch'u bonds with its subordinate states, for there was no point in remaining allied with a loser.

Overall, the historical backdrop to Sun Tzu's work—the tense and chaotic Spring and Autumn period—saw a new emphasis on rational planning rather than traditional, symbolic kowtowing. In an era when no higher authority could be taken for granted and everyone was forced to look out for themselves, Sun Tzu formulated ways to wield one's own power through strategic thinking. Formal appearances become less important than getting the job done in Machiavellian fashion—through whatever means possible.

In short, effectiveness—results—became the standard by which things were judged, rather than ceremony and obedience to appropriate forms of behavior. Yet in all of this, Sun Tzu maintained a reverence for fundamental Chinese virtues of moderation, foresight, and self-control. He didn't so much depart from traditional Chinese spirituality as retool it to fit a new political and military landscape. He responded to the chaos of his era with a way of imposing order not through grand symbolic ideas of virtue, but through acting as individuals, as cool-headed, self-accountable, free-thinking masters of our own fates.

A BRIEF HISTORY

The 2,000-Year Bestseller

Originally a secret publication for an emperor's eyes alone, *The Art of War* has become popular reading for millions.

○ ○ ○

THE ORIGINAL APPEARANCE of *The Art of War* in ancient China around 500 B.C. can't be called a publication in the modern sense of the word. Sun Tzu wasn't writing for a reading public but for the eyes of the emperor Ho-lü and his successors only. While the circumstances of its composition are unclear, it seems fairly certain that *The Art of War* was written by Sun Wu, brilliant strategist and general in Ho-lü's army who was instrumental in the conquest of Ch'u by the kingdom of Wu.

As in the case of other, earlier Chinese military manuals (such as the anonymously penned *Six Secret Teachings*), state authorities zealously guarded *The Art of War*. In fact, possession of such a manuscript was considered a serious offense. The manuscript was passed down among the ruling classes of China for centuries. Even today, archaeological digs at sites near the major centers of ancient Chinese civilization continue to unearth copies of the manuscript.

Yet the appeal of *The Art of War* in Asia was not limited to China alone. A millennium after its first appearance in Wu, it entered the canon of Japanese and Korean military lore as well. In Japan especially, its fame was vast. Any Japanese military ruler worth his salt was expected to know Sun Tzu well.

The Western world's exposure to *The Art of War* dates back to 1782, when a Jesuit missionary named Père Amiot rendered Sun Tzu's manuscript into French. For Amiot, who had no military background or interests,

51

The Art of War

the work was chiefly a museum piece, a historical curiosity. But soon afterward, a minor French military officer discovered Amiot's translation and discerned Sun Tzu's brilliance as a strategist. The officer circulated *The Art of War* among the literate French military elite until it eventually found its way into the hands of none other than the Emperor Napoleon Bonaparte.

Napoleon appears to have read Sun Tzu's work with some care, although it's impossible to verify the legend that he actually carried it into battle with him. Regardless, the story of Napoleon's reliance on Sun Tzu—along with the notion that *The Art of War* was the secret to Napoleon's meteoric rise to power—became inextricably tied up with the work. If Napoleon did pore over *The Art of War* as intensively as myth has it, his defeat at Waterloo is ironic, because he made a tactical error that Sun Tzu explicitly warned against in his segment on knowing the terrain. Napoleon's nemesis, the British general Wellington, had his troops lie low in the furrows of a vast rolling field. When they appeared, Napoleon ordered an advance—rather than the retreat that Sun Tzu recommends.

The Art of War didn't appear in an English version until 1905, when a British military officer translated it. A small circle of predominantly military men studied the work, but the translation was arcane and attracted no more than a passing interest. But Sun Tzu's work received a major boost in fame five years later, in 1910, when the distinguished Sinologist Lionel Giles—co-creator of the Wade-Giles transliteration system for writing Chinese words in the English alphabet—retranslated it. Giles, an assistant curator at the British Museum, was able not only to translate the military terms as the 1905 translation had done, but to insert the work more fully into the cultural and historical context of China. Giles was able to shed light on the Taoist background of *The Art of War* and to relate Sun Tzu's work to the spiritual and philosophical tradition of China much more clearly. Still, Giles was a museum curator rather than a military man, and some gaps showed in his expertise in Chinese culture when he tried to convey Sun Tzu's intricate strategy suggestions. Giles's training in warfare wasn't quite up to the task, and there are spots of unintelligibility in his translation.

The next English translation, however, rectified this problem of military inarticulacy. It appeared in 1963, courtesy of Samuel Griffith, a brigadier general in the United States Marine Corps, who, not surprisingly, had a great deal of military experience under his belt. Appearing as it did

A Brief History

at the height of the Cold War, just after the Cuban missile crisis, Griffith's translation of Sun Tzu struck a nerve. The work found a widespread audience that it had never enjoyed before. Diplomats, military leaders, and political scientists were suddenly interested in its practical, hands-on approach to strategy formulation. At the same time, *The Art of War* began to attract laypeople as it never had before, though Griffith's awkward English style did put off some mainstream readers.

Several more fluent and readable English translations of *The Art of War* appeared in the following decades. But the real galvanizing jolt to Sun Tzu's work came with a 1983 translation that featured an introductory commentary by the popular historical novelist James Clavell. Though Clavell didn't translate the work himself, his editors drew upon the marketability of his name by putting him on the cover. Clavell's bestselling novel *Shogun* (1975), had aroused widespread American popular interest in ancient Asian warrior culture. The marketing ploy of attaching Clavell's name to *The Art of War* worked, and the new translation became something of a sensation.

Sun Tzu's work also gained new fame in the context of Japan's rise as a major economic power in the late 1970s and early 1980s. Many Western businessmen regarded Japanese culture—and more generally, the "Asian work ethic"—with envy and awe. A spate of works appeared that applied Japanese ideas to American management strategies and business theory. *The Art of War*, though Chinese in origin, was seen to fit snugly among them, and it was effectively retooled as a manual for businesspeople.

The business world continues to provide the main market for copies of *The Art of War* today. Both Japanese and American corporate executives continue to read it widely, and it appears on syllabi of numerous MBA programs at graduate business schools. One writer, Gary Gagliardi, has turned Sun Tzu into a veritable industry of his own, churning out a series of business books that apply *The Art of War* to various aspects of entrepreneurship, including sales, marketing, and management.

It's hard to imagine how Sun Tzu would react to the conversion of his military manual into a business guide. But it's likely that, given his practical mind and appreciation for material results, he would give his contemporary business readers a thumbs-up.

EXPLORE

Other Books of Interest

Interested in learning more about Sun Tzu? There's plenty to read, ranging from the academic to the thoroughly practical.

○ ○ ○

IN OUR DAY, AT LEAST, businesspeople comprise by far the biggest group of Sun Tzu's readers. Executives, CEOs, and mid-level managers turn to the Chinese theorist for lessons about strategy that might bear fruit in the contemporary business scene. Beginning in the 1980s, when an American fascination with Japanese work culture blossomed, a slew of books appeared that draw corporate lessons from Japanese leadership styles. Because Japanese executives have long valued *The Art of War* as a corporate textbook, these works indirectly show the powerful influence of Sun Tzu. There are far too many of these business treatises to list completely, but major titles among them include *Kaizen Strategies for Successful Leadership* by Tony Barnes (Pitman Publishing, 1996), *Shogun Management* by William C. Byham (HarperBusiness, 1993), and *American Samurai* by William Lareau (TimeWarner, 1991).

More recently, a business writer named Gary Gagliardi has created a cottage industry in applying Sun Tzu's work to specifically defined domains of the business world, ranging from marketing to sales to management. These books are valuable in the detailed applications they bring to the insights of *The Art of War*, which at times comes across as infuriatingly vague. Gagliardi's works include *The Art of War Plus the Art of Sales: An Adaptation for Sales People* (Clearbridge Publishing, 1999), *The Art of War Plus the Art of Management: An Adaptation for Managers* (Clearbridge Publishing, 1999), and *The Art of War Plus the Art of Marketing: An Adaptation for Marketing People* (Clearbridge Publishing, 1999).

The Art of War

Taking a more academic tack, one useful way to expand an understanding of *The Art of War* is to explore the time and culture in which Sun Tzu lived. For the ambitious, the three-volume *Cambridge History of China*, edited by Denis Twitchett and John K. Fairbank (1979–1986) is unparalleled in completeness. But those of us who lack the patience for that magisterial work can find a shorter survey in the first volume of *East Asia: The Great Tradition* by Edwin O. Reischauer and John K. Fairbank (1958). For those interested in the political science aspect of the institution of the king in ancient China, the classic resource is *The Origins of Statecraft in China: The Western Chou Empire* (1970) by Herrlee G. Creel. A more compact introduction to the Chinese ideas about statecraft—both those influenced by Sun Tzu and those not—appears in *The Art of Rulership* (1983) by Roger Ames.

Some specialized works on Chinese culture can help flesh out the cultural background of *The Art of War*. For example, Sun Tzu doesn't expound very much on the intricacies of the Chinese state. For a thorough study of the important role of the bureaucrat in Chinese culture and how the emperor was occasionally under their influence, see *Chinese Civilization and Bureaucracy* (1964) by Etienne Balazs. This heavy-duty scholarly work is useful in providing a perspective on the vast and complex institution of Chinese bureaucracy that Sun Tzu almost totally ignores in *The Art of War*. And for a better understanding of the geography of China, *A Geography of China* (1965) by T.R. Tregear provides an invaluable resource.

One of the most interesting aspects of *The Art of War* is its spiritual dimension. Readers interested in the role of Taoism in Sun Tzu can find a good and readable introduction to the thought of Lao-tzu in *The Way and its Power* (1958) by Arthur Waley. A shorter overview of Lao-tzu's thought appears in *The Way of Lao-tzu* (1963) by Chan Wing-tsit. While neither of these works focus on Sun Tzu or *The Art of War* in particular, they offer a good discussion of ideas about the Tao that were in the air in China in Sun Tzu's day and help illuminate his sometimes perplexing use of the word Tao. For an introduction to Confucianism, another spiritual development more or less contemporary with Sun Tzu, see *The Analects of Confucius* (1938) by Arthur Waley. Confucius was a very different thinker from Sun Tzu, and in some ways his polar opposite, as in his emphasis on the importance of virtue in all areas of public life—a view that the ethically uninterested Sun Tzu would have rejected outright.